Bear went downtown by
himself. The sidewalk was
crowded with shoppers.

Bear saw something on the
sidewalk. He picked it up. It
was a baton!

Bear walked along, waving
the baton.

Soon everyone began to march behind Bear! When he went left, they went left.

When the light changed and
Bear stopped, they stopped.

More marchers hurried to
join the parade. Was it because
of Bear or the baton? No one
could say for sure.

The parade went past Fox's Department Store. Barb Fox came out. "Bear," she said, "I'd like you to lead Fox's Thanksgiving Day Parade."

And that's just what Bear did!